YOU CALL, I'LL DRIVE
J.D. Phillippi

Copyright © 2019 J.D. Phillippi
All rights reserved.
ISBN:
ISBN-13:

To Donna.

Always, to Donna.

To all my riders.

**You Call,
I Drive**

Stories From The Rideshare Industry

By
   J.D. Phillippi

CHAPTER ONE
The Official Stuff

You Call, I Drive
> Stories From the Rideshare Industry

by J.D. Phillippi

Copyright 2019

All rights reserved. No part of this publication may be reproduced, stored in a retrieval system or transmitted in any form or by any means - electronic, mechanical, photocopy, recording or any other - except for brief quotations in printed reviews, without the prior permission of the publisher.

All persons in this book are fictional. Any resemblance to persons living or dead is entirely coincidental.

Cover Design by Phlipside Creative

CHAPTER TWO
Introduction

Light plays across the dashboard of my car. Splashes of red, blue, yellow, green or white slide through the passenger compartment, then glide away leaving me in darkness. During the day, the view in my windows and mirrors changes. Cars and trucks move in and out of view. The sun rises, traffic lights bring a little order to the intricate, competitive ballet of city traffic. The light fades as the sun sets and the lights illuminate my world again.

I enjoy driving. Being behind the wheel of a nice car feels good. But it's more than that. Maybe I watch too many movies, but the view through the windshield fascinates me. The entire world held within the frame of my windshield. My universe becomes what is visible in the windows or the mirrors. It strikes me as very cinematic, especially when you add in the mystery of a silhouette in the back seat. Conversations in the dark feed into the atmosphere of driving for me. Daylight driving is more energized because you can see everything, and there's much more going on. More cars, more pedestrians, more movement. Nights can get busy, especially on the weekends. Add to the mystique of the lighting doors opening and closing, with loud conversation from the groups of people who pile in and out of the car.

Bet you didn't know there was a kind of poetry in all this, did you?

There is some social scienceas well. Driving for hour after hour will give you a solid look at how people behave. Far too often, it's not pretty.

Why do I drive? There's nothing romantic about that answer. For the last two years, I have been "under-employed". That's the official terminology for someone who is making less money than they need to pay their bills or is working below their level of experience or training. In my case, both. I moved here for a job five years ago. Through a variety of circumstances, the job and I parted company (I've left jobs on worse terms, but unemployed is unemployed). While the resumes and applications flowed I needed something to help pay the bills. And driving for a rideshare company offered flexibility and easy money. So I downloaded the app, jumped through the hoops and got rolling.

Over the last two years, I have worked for both of the major players in this field. Overall, they are about even. They are not identical, but they have more upside than down. I have nothing bad to say about either.

Well, OK. There is ONE thing I'd like to file a small complaint about against both. The navigation system can be a pain in the ass. Some frustrating quirks that I describe later. I've talked to riders and other drivers who report the same issues, so I know it's not me. Note to the powers that be and all their programming geniuses, a fix on this one would be appreciated!

Other than that, my time as a ride-share driver has been good. I'm not getting rich, but the money I make is keeping the wolf from the door. I have not had a "bad" rider, so far. So far. Now I've probably jinxed myself! I enjoy being around people, I inherited my mother's ability to talk to anyone and my father's love of driving. Along with a reliable car that's what you need to succeed in this industry. Beyond those basics, I would include problem-solving (what do you do when the indicated route is closed for repair or an accident?). I guarantee you will have unexpected problems pop up. How you deal with them makes a huge difference in your success and your ratings from your riders.

While all that is going on outside, here's some of what is happening inside the car. Stories that are funny and sad and sometimes a little risque. More than a few riders have heard some of these and urged me to write them down. So here they are. I hope you enjoy the ride.

CHAPTER THREE
Behind The Wheel

If I'm writing a book about what happens inside a rideshare vehicle, I suppose I can't omit the driver. I don't claim that what follows covers all the drivers of all the services. In the course of the last couple years, I've met a few drivers along the way. Even from that small sample size, I will say that we are a diverse group with a wide range of motivation. So let's just stick to your driver of the moment.

Me. A college-educated man of, ahem, "late middle age" who has been a dishwasher, shuttle bus driver, parking lot attendant, bellhop, muffin baker, radio DJ, copywriter, newscaster, youth minister, substitute teacher, audiobook narrator, and rideshare driver. Married to his college sweetheart and father of a grown child. Bicyclist, photographer, and author. Call those the high points.

This was never on my radar of possible career moves. I mentioned in the Introduction that I started driving when I lost a full-time job. The job had brought us to a new city in a part of the country where we had almost no connections. Most of the people I knew at the end of two years there were people from work. That meant that I not only lost my job but most of my social circle too. That's a scary, scary place to find yourself at my age. My tradition is to give myself a little time to mourn, to feel sorry for myself when bad things happen. Once that time has passed, then it's time to figure out what's next.

There were two options that popped up quickly. The first was working as a substitute teacher in the local school district. You didn't have to be a certified teacher, just have a college degree. So I began the approval process of the district. That would not be enough to keep our heads above water, so I needed to look for other ways to make more money.

Enter the rideshare industry. Here's was a chance to earn income on whatever schedule worked for me! Jobs available 24/7/365. Work full-time or as a side gig. So it was a second job that fit perfectly with the substitute teaching. I started each of the jobs within a month of each other.

Most days, I work till 2 or 3 in the afternoon at school (it depends on whether I'm at a middle school or high school. They get out at different times), then move directly into driving. So I'm in my "teacher" clothes when I'm rideshare driving. So far, I haven't had a pickup at the school where I taught that day, but it's possible. I have picked up parents, teachers and older students at other schools. Because I teach in a suburban school district, my first move is to drive into Richmond. It's not that there aren't rides out there, but the drive between pick-ups is longer, and I can make more money, faster by working in the city. My goal is to make $30-50 before 6 PM. If I can do that, the bills get paid (in combination with my sub pay, and the income from the rest of my family).

Most drivers have a goal. It may be daily or weekly. It may be hours or dollars. I have been a rider twice so far and chatted with my fellow drivers. One gentleman had figured out how much he needed to make each day to cover the expenses of his car (loan payment, gas, and maintenance) and increase his overall income by the amount he wanted. If I remember correctly, it was $100 a day. So he drove as long as it took him to make that amount. Some days that was eight hours, some days it was twelve. It becomes a "you gotta do what you gotta do" kind of job. Twelve hours in a car, no matter how nice, is a long day. I have a total income per week goal that I need to hit. How much I drive changes based on how many days of substitute teaching I get. Which means I do a lot more driving in the summer than during the school year!

So my schedule looks like this: Monday-Thursday I drive approximately three hours a day. I can hit my daily goal easily during the 2 PM to 6 PM hours. They are some of the highest demand hours of the day. Friday and Saturday, I drive in the evening. Lots of people going out to dinner, bars, plays, concerts, whatever. Using a rideshare saves them from finding a parking space, paying for that parking space, hassling with traffic before and after the event, and being able to relax and have a good time. My rule is that I do not drive after midnight. The level of stupid and the likelihood that I will have a problem balloons after midnight. I can make plenty of money and avoid the nonsense by quitting sometimeduring the 11 o'clock hour. The only exception to this rule is New Year's Eve. The busiest hour of the night is midnight to 1 AM. The people going home at that hour are usually OK, so I grab the extra income as I can.

When you get in my car, a couple of things always happen. I will always check to make sure you are the correct rider. That saves both of us a hassle. I will greet you, often asking how your day is going. How much we talk after that is mostly up to you. If I have questions, I will ask them then. I usually check if the trip has multiple stops. People will get them out of order sometimes. Checking on the first stop before we leave makes everyone's day easier. When you leave my car, you may notice that I look behind me. That's making sure you have everything. Having to deal with stuff left behind is a hassle and it keeps me from making money. I will also wish you a great day/evening. My hope is that the ride was a pleasant one for you and that your day will get even bettermoving forward. It makes me a little sad how often that wish is met by surprise. I do what I can to make the world a little more pleasant a place.

As I mention elsewhere, one of the most common questions I get is "Do you like (driving)?" By andlarge,the answer is yes. There are days when things are better than others. The great thing about this job is that if the day is being stupid, I can just go home. Some days are slow. After hours of driving, I'm just burning gas and adding mileage to the car. I go home. If the traffic is filled with people trying to kill me, I go home. I'll make up the shortfall somewhere else and it will be fine. I enjoy driving, and the challenge of problem-solving that comes with it. Most trips are short, which means I'm always getting a new situation to keep my brain occupied. That's the way I like things. Last, but not least, I like people. Some are more pleasant than others, but overall my riders have been great people. I've had some fun conversations and met some interesting people. I enjoy being a cheerleader for my new hometown as well.

So for as long as I need to do, I'll keep doing it.

And when the need arises:

You call, I drive.

CHAPTER FOUR
The Challenges

This job is pretty simple. Simple enough for the title of a book! You call, I drive. That's the essence of the whole program. My role is to achieve three things:

- Get you to your destination safely. Your safety, my safety, and the safety of everyone around us is the single most important part of the process.

- Get you there comfortably. I won't sacrifice comfort for safety but you should be able to focus on other things than how I'm driving.

- Get you there efficiently. Some folks might want to move this to the #2 slot, but I'm don't. Efficiency is important to both rider and driver. You want to get to your destination with as little delay as possible. And I want to give as many rides per hour as I can. That's how I make the best money. But if being efficient diminishes our safety or your comfort, I put it third.

Since my job is to get people where they want to go quickly and safely, I am always on l lookout for folks doing things that will get in the way of that aim. At the top of the list are:

The **video game drivers** - I am not one of the "blame video games for everything" crowd. At the same time, too many drivers seem to feel that they are scoring points in a game, and looking to collect prizes by racing through traffic. Don't forget, I'm driving in an urban setting. Downtown streets, residential areas. There are delivery trucks stopped to make a pickup or a drop-off. Pedestrians, children and small animals. What always fascinates me is the number of times someone goes blowing by me, only to end up right next to me at the next traffic light. Simple math will tell you that the extra speed you are using will result in an inconsequential difference to your arrival time. And if you get ticketed, you will be much later. I hope everyone won't take offense, but I drive with the assumption that everyone on the road is an idiot. This protects me from the actual idiots, and gives me regular pleasant surprises when drivers are safe and sane.

Speaking of **pedestrians**... sigh. Let me spell out the physics of this. The average person weighs around 160 pounds, let's say. The average car weighs over a ton (2,000 pounds). So it wouldn't matter if you weighed two or even three times the average, you will lose against any vehicle on the road. Yet I still see pedestrians acting as if their desire to cross a street makes the laws of physics disappear. You may have the legal right of way, but as my father used to say, you can be right all the way to the emergency room. People cross at unwise times or unwise places. I do so love it when they pop out from between parked cars! Or when they take their own sweet time to get from point A to point B. I understand that not everyone can move fast. That's not who I'm talking about. I had a pedestrian cross in the middle of the block and cross the street on a diagonal, making the time they were in the street as long as possible. All this done at what I would call an "amble". Worse yet, it was at night and they were in dark clothing. I came around a corner and had to stop dead to let him finish the cross. My reward was a look that implied I was interfering with his life. Sigh. Seriously folks, I don't want to hit you any more than you want me to hit you. Let's work together on this.

With that in mind, let's take a moment to talk about **smartphones**. No, let's not, I'll just get riled. Crossing a street with your nose in your smartphone is a fantastic way to get killed. It amazes me that it doesn't happen more often. I refuse to believe that you are doing anything so important that it can't wait till you're in a safe place. Smartphones are great in the right time and place. The whole ride share system wouldn't work without them. I love my smartphone, but it stays in my pocket until

I need it. Walking in an urban environment surrounded by vehicles that can't deny physics isn't a place for them.

Bicyclists. Time to pick on my own tribe. I have been biking, on and off, for about 50 years. My new home is bike friendly, and I enjoy urban riding. But the number of times I want to pull over and scream at my fellow cyclists is astounding. It goes beyond the simple concept of "Always wear a helmet" (I am hardcore on this subject). It protects everything of importance inside your skull that makes you you. I have fallen off my bike a couple times and my helmet protected my essential me-ness. Riding carelessly in an environment surrounded by vehicles that outweigh you by multiple orders of magnitude is stupid. Under the best circumstances, you only have a limited number of options if things go bad on an urban ride.

What amazes is me is that everything that a pedestrian can do wrong seems to multiply for some of my fellow cyclists. I have watched more than a few folks on bikes roll through red lights without a glance to the right or the left. First, that's illegal. Red means stop for two wheeled, human powered vehicles like everyone else. Second, the number of drivers I see blowing through intersections, often against red lights, is frightening. No signaling stops or turns, random lane changes, swerving in between vehicles, going the wrong way on one-way streets. Again, I'm amazed I don't see more accidents than I do, but there are plenty of little memorials scattered around the city to fatal bike accidents.

Parallel Parking. We all suck at it. Enough said.

The upside of the job is that I get to watch a beautiful city roll by. Sometimes I get to drive out into the rolling countryside that surrounds the city. It's a cool view. Plus, I get to meet some of the amazing people who live here.

CHAPTER FIVE
Your Best Story

There are three questions I get asked all the time:
How long have you been driving?
So you're from Pittsburgh?
What's your best driving story?

The answer to the first question keeps changing. As of the moment I'm writing this, it's around two-and-a-halfyears.

For the second, it's "Born and raised".

Ah, but the third. There is only one story to answer that question. I will share it with you in a second.

I am sure that every driver has several stories that fit the bill. With 2,000+ riders through my car, I have met all kinds of people. Most of them have been fine. But some of them? Well, let's say they are the inspiration for this entire book.

At the top of the list of stories is the one I call "Not Getting It". Among the fantasies of most men, I will bet you find the one where the woman (or whoever) can't wait any longer to have wild, passionate sex. It's the "tearing my clothes off my body" fantasy.

Hmmm, you may be getting the wrong idea already. No clothes were removed during this ride. By anyone.

It was well into the evening when my phone pinged with this ride. The sun had been down for about three hours. I pulled up outside a local hot-spot to let a young couple climb in the back. A young man and a young woman, both of whom were making a wise decision to let someone else drive that night. Both were slurring their words a little and were having a little trouble focusing. One more than the other.

They got in and I did my thing. The drive was only about five minutes and a couple of miles. As I worked my way through the nighttime traffic, my ears picked up that two different conversations seemed to be taking place in the back seat.

The young man was offering a long, wandering monologue on a wide range of subjects. I'm not sure what the central concept was, but he seemed very interested in it. He wasn't intense about it but he was persistent.

On the other hand, the young lady had a single idea in mind. It began with a question.

"Do you want me?"

OK, so this was one of those conversations I DON'T want to listen in on. None of my business. I'm hoping that people can keep it to intellectual concepts until I can get them home. In the quick glimpse I had gotten of my passengers, they both seemed like attractive enough young people. So the outcome of the conversation seemed obvious enough.

As I mentioned, these folks had been drinking for a while based on their condition. Like a lot of drunk people, they don't really comprehend how loud they are talking. That exaggerated "whisper-that-isn't-a-whisper" thing. That's what was going on in the back seat. She was trying to keep it between them, but her alcohol inhibited hearing was letting her down.

On the other hand, he was paying her no attention at all. He continued to ramble on to other unrelated subjects without pause. So she tried again.

"I want you."

And he rambled on.

"I want you to touch me."

Nope, Oblivious Boy kept on with his semi-mumbled discussion with himself.

"You can have me when we get home."

YOU CALL, I DRIVE 17

At this point, my eyes are getting big, and I'm wondering what is about to happen in my backseat. I'm also screaming inside my head "WHAT IS WRONG WITH YOU, DUDE?"

Seriously, how drunk do you have to be that when an attractive person snuggles up next to you (I could see their silhouettes very close together in my rear-view mirror) and makes very clear their sexual desire for you, you somehow can remain utterly unaware? I don't ever want to be that drunk.)

This goes on minute after minute. She keeps trying to get him interested, while he is living in some bizarre world of his own creation. At this point, his conversation seemed to change. Now he was talking about what they could do in their apartment, rearranging things and changing the layout.

The young lady finally had enough. I could hear her shift in her seat so she was looking right at him. As I got to the block with their drop off address, she made herself clear.

"I want to f*ck."

It was all I could do not to burst out laughing. It's that fantasy moment. When the object of your desire matches or even exceeds your own level of excitement. Surely, this would snap our young hero back into the moment, and at just the right time.

Nope.

I swear to you, he started talking about setting up a volleyball net in the living room. He was certain there was enough space and then they'd have a net right there any time they needed it.

"I don't want to play volleyball, I want to f*ck!"

With that final statement, I rolled up to the small house at the address indicated by the app. The young man still seemed to have no idea of what was happening right next to him, managing to stumble out of the car. She slid semi-gracefully out after him, wrapped an arm around his waist and they moved off toward the house. After doing a quick check to make sure they had not left anything (ANYTHING) behind, I put the car in gear and rolled off. I could only shake my head at the young guy. If he was lucky, she would tear off his clothes and have her way with him as soon as they walked through the door.

Either that or he would wake up to a very unhappy lady in the morning.

I will be honest, I have no idea which way I would lay odds for him.

That is easily my "best" story and my favorite. I know it is a favorite of the ladies who have heard it. It would seem, gentlemen, that more than a few of us need to work on our listening skills.

CHAPTER SIX
Loud Women

I have a favorite group of passengers. It's probably wrong to play favorites but what can I say? There is one category of passenger that brings a smile to my face every time I see them waiting for me.

Rowdy women.

When I see a group of women outside a bar, club or restaurant with that certain vibe going, I know it will be a fun ride. They're laughing and everything about their body language says that they are having a good time. And they have no intention of settling down for the dude driving the car.

I love it.

I had my first experience of rowdy female passengers early on with a group of college-aged women. Four of them hopped into the car with presents, and mylar balloons in tow. The young lady sitting upfront with me (and the balloons) apologized in advance, saying it was her birthday and her "squad" was in party mode. I told her that was fine with me and off we went. Over the last two years, I've had several more groups of female rowdies and enjoyed every one of them.

One group asked me for my best story, so I told them one I've shared here. That drew gales of laughter, followed by some merciless dissection of various men in their lives. Male "locker room talk" tends toward the sledgehammer. When the ladies start in, it is steely sharp knives that slash deep. And one particular gentleman was sliced and diced with great zeal on this trip.

The younger rowdies bring an astounding energy level to the car. But the older ladies bring a self-assurance that only comes with experience. They always apologize for their language or the topic, but I laugh and tell them to be themselves. Because "themselves" is such an amazing experience. They all tend to "warn" me they will be loud. I smile and welcome them to my car.

I am asked by all age groups if I'm married. Married for 37 years and with the same woman for over 40. Those numbers usually impress them. When I add that I married my college sweetheart, I am guaranteed to get an "Awwwww". As much as my male ego would love to believe that's a response to my charming personality and good looks, I know it there is a different question coming. Some variation of "So what do you think about…?" Usually some guy's failure to do what the ladies think he ought. I will stand by my brothers as much as I can, but there have been occasions when the infraction described was so wrong that I agreed with the ladies. I had one woman ask if I'd be willing to repeat my answer on the phone to her husband.

I declined. What am I, stupid?

Again, the difference between rowdy men and rowdy women is straightforward. The guys are obscene and repetitive. Yeah, I heard your opinion of the women in your lives the first five times. It wasn't interesting or creative any of those times. But the ladies? Oh, my. The creativity of their descriptions, the withering criticism, the carefree bawdiness of some of these groups is such a blast.

Some folks may be tut-tutting right now. That's not the way "ladies" are to behave. Honestly, I've had fewer problems with women than men. A man will occasionally become aggressive, though never towards me. The ladies are all about the group they're with. At worst (or best), I'm just a plaything along the way of their party. And I am happy to play my part.

CHAPTER SEVEN
Cancellations

Cancellations are another inevitable part of the rideshare life. They can happen for a lot of reasons. Some of them I understand while others are a source of extreme irritation. There can be some unfortunate gamesmanship involved which I find offensive at a profound level.

What's going on with cancellations? There are a lot of answers to that question. Sometimes I show up sooner than expected. If you figure you will be ready to leave in about ten minutes, and it usually takes ten minutes for your driver to show up, you make the call ten minutes before you're ready to go. That's being efficient for everyone. The problem arises when I'm around the corner when you make the request and I show up less than sixty seconds later. That doesn't work for anyone. Like most drivers, I hate waiting. I'm not making any money at that point. Yes, I'll make money if you take longer than the programmed wait time in the system, but it's a pittance. They set the system up so you can cancel in the first couple minutes without penalty, and while annoying to the driver, it can be better for everyone if you do.

On the other hand, I have driven several minutes, been just around the corner from the destination and had someone cancel. Since I don't know what happened at the other end (medical emergency, a big fight with the significant other, whatever) I suppose I should be reasonable about this one. It's annoying and cost me both time and money.

Now, what about this game playing I mentioned?

If you cancel after the allotted time, they charge you a cancellation fee. That's being fair to the driver who gave up their time and whatever earnings they might have made, to head your way. Trust me, drivers believe we miss out on long, profitable trips with another rider every time we get canceled. I've heard a couple of riders complain about having to pay such a fee. They believed they should be able to drop a ride for any reason at no charge. Please remember, whether it's for extra spending money or as a primary job, all your drivers are trying to make money. We are real people, putting our personal vehicles at your disposal. That doesn't make us servants. Treat me fairly and I will treat you fairly. Making a ride request is the first step in a social contract. You call, I'll drive. If you break your end of the contract, then there's a penalty. If I cancel, I'm penalized too. It goes against the all-important ride acceptance rating. The window on that rating is small, and if I fall below that line, my right to work with that service gets suspended.

There is a game that some drivers play that I have no respect forwhatsoever. They accept a request, see where the pickup is and decide they don't want that ride. If the driver cancels at that point, they will suffer. So what they do is drive aimlessly, usually in the opposite direction of the rider. If you text or call them, they will tell you they can't find you, the navigation system is malfunctioning, whatever. What they want is for you to cancel. It frees them from the ride they don't want and they pick up your cancellation fee. As far as I am concerned,this is dishonest and unethical. I have no respect for a driver that would do this. As I discuss elsewhere in this book, I drive in every single neighborhood in my city and the surrounding suburbs. If I accept a ride, I will do everything I can to live up to that commitment. That includes one surprise trip that had a four hour round trip.

I want to note that sometimes your driver is not being a jerk, just struggling. I had a rider cancel on me because they saw me driving around in circles. It was during summer construction season and new projects and detours seemed to pop up daily. I was on one side of a major street and the rider was a coupleof blocks on the other. The way navigation sent me had a huge construction project blocking my path. The next route I chose was clear to the major street, but I had forgotten I couldn't cross at that point. A couple more poor choices/new detours and I am certain that the rider thought I was an idiot. They canceled the ride and I understand. One of us should have contacted the other to see what was happening, but sometimes that doesn't happen.

My least favorite cancellation involves me going above and beyond, and the rider not doing likewise.

I was west of the city, out in the suburbs, when I got a ping for a longish trip (15+ minutes to the pickup). The night had been slow, so I was taking whatever came my way. This trip was even further west, out into the countryside. I worked my way through the unlit back roads, making my way to the long dark driveway, out in the middle of nowhere. These always make me a little nervous. Not because anything has ever happened but because I watch way too many cop shows and have a vivid imagination. I pull up to the house and wait. There is not a single interior light lit that I can see.

You might think the dark house was a giveaway that there was a problem, but it's not true in my experience. A lot of the houses seem to have the living spaces on the backside of the building. Which means the family or whoever can be active inside, but the front of the house looks abandoned. The things you learn along the way, lol!

So I sat there through the standard waiting period and then sent the text message. "Hi, this is your driver. I'm waiting out front of the house". A minute later, I get a response.

"What house?"

Uh oh.

I send the address via text again.

The phone rings.

"That's my house."

Yes, ma'am. I'm here to pick you up.

"I'm not there, I'm at my club."

Turns out the rider was back in the opposite direction, at a club outside the city limits. In other words, about 40 minutes away from where I was, but only about 15 from where I had started. My best bet is that they put their destination in as the pickup address. I politely suggested that they change the address and I would be there as soon as I could. She hung up. And canceled the ride. So I was now facing 40+ minutes of non-earning time. All because someone couldn't handle the app. Lovely.

I made the standard $5 for the cancellation.

I was not a happy camper on the way home.

In the end, if you have to cancel, go ahead andcancel. All I'm asking is that you remember there is a human being at the other end of the app. That goes for riders and drivers alike.

CHAPTER EIGHT
Flat Tire in the Rain

In the time I've been driving, I have been fortunate. I've never had a "bad" rider. No one who was abusive, destructive or otherwise objectionable. I've never had a bad experience picking someone up or letting them off. I've never had an accident. Driving has been uneventful on the larger scale.

Which doesn't mean that I have had no adventures at all.

Bad weather is a challenge for most people, but is a gift for a ride share driver. Doesn't matter if it's rain or snow, it's a problem when you need a ride. Most of us don't want to get soaked, or slog through snow, or overheat in the summer sun. So we look for other ways to get where we want to go. Calling your favorite ride share app is a quick and easy way to get around when the weather is being a problem. So I tend to be cheerful on those dreary, cold, wet days.

There is one exception in my otherwise incident free ride history. The day in question featured a heavy rain. Not a light drizzle or a steady rain, but a downpour, hour after hour. What I call "Noah, build an ark" weather. The gutters were awash, and business was good. The ride in question had nothing to mark it as different from hundreds of others. Pick up the rider after work and drop them off at home. One side of town to the other. It was a ride that would take fewer than 10 minutes under normal circumstances.

One of the realities of working in a city that's been around for several centuries is that some side streets are narrow. Add in cars parked along the curb and the margins for two cars to slip by one another can be slim. Just blocks after the pickup I came to one of those side streets. There was another car coming the opposite direction, so I tried to stay as close to my side of the road as possible. Turns out it was too close. I felt my right rear tire clip the curb and apologized to my rider for the bump. Two blocks later and I knew I had a problem.

There is an unmistakable sound and feel to a tire going flat. I made it far enough to get to a major intersection where there was a lot more room to maneuver. I pulled over to the right into what was a "No Parking" zone and stared out the window. The weather outside continued to drench my universe without a care that I had to get out of the car. That I had to get out of the car and spend some considerable time outside. I knew I had a flat tire before the car came to a stop. I knew changing this tire in these conditions would be unpleasant. Unpleasant and long.

My next step was to turn around and tell my rider that they might want to cancel my trip and call another driver. We discussed how long I thought changing the tire would take versus how long the wait might be for another driver. I told her she was welcome to stay inside the car till another car arrived. After considering it, she decided to stick with me. I told her to hang tight and that I'd get this done as quick as I could.

A little background about my father is useful here. My dad was a "car guy". By that I mean he covered his high school notebooks in doodles of car designs. He did all kinds of car repairs himself, starting at a young age. He was a gearhead. Over the course of his life, my father owned 100+ cars. I never got a complete, definitive count. Big cars, little cars, fast cars, family cars, station wagons, sports cars, you name it. He once owned a car made out of two different cars. Not even the same model! The front end was one thing, and the rear was another. So the one thing he required of his children was that before we could drive his cars, we needed to understand how they worked. That meant knowing how to change a tire, change the oil, name the major systems of the vehicle (power, suspension, steering, brakes, drive train) and know how a four-stroke internal combustion engine worked. I helped him bleed brake lines, and replace an engine that one of my brothers had broken. It was fundamental to my life behind the wheel.

So changing the tire was a walk in the park. I've done it several times at the side of the road.

But never in the pouring rain.

I hit the button to pop the trunk and climbed out. My rider asked if I wanted her to hold an umbrella or something. I declined. There was no point in both of us getting wet, and there was no way I was going to avoid getting drenched. A quick look at the right rear tire confirmed my fears. Flat as a pancake. Later examination showed that I had sliced the sidewall when I hit the curb. So now to retrieve the spare and the jack from the trunk. Of course, holding them down was a wing nut on a long bolt. A nut that hadn't moved in years and was tight and hard to budge. That means I was soaked before I even get started. I wrestle them both out, setting the modern limited use spare against the bumper.

Now for the fun part. I have to get the scissor jack in the right spot under the rocker panel (that's the part of the body under the doors). The only way to do that is on your hands and knees. Did I mention the gutters were awash? My estimate is that there was three inches of water ripping along where I had to kneel. Plus I dress in business casual when I drive, so this was a pair of khakis forced to double as work pants.

Picture this in your mind. I've been out in the torrent for about four minutes. My hair is soaked, rain covering my glasses, dripping off my nose and chin. Shoes? Squishing. Pants? From mid-thigh down, soaked. Shirt is sticking to my back from collar to belt. I loosen the lug nuts on the wheel while it's still on the ground, crank the scissor jack till the wheel comes off the ground, and finish removing the nuts. Still raining. I set the lug nuts down by my knee, to keep track of them. Off comes the old wheel. If you've never changed a tire, let me tell you this - tires on steel wheels are heavy. Especially while you're on your knees. Soaking wet. In the pouring rain, in a gutter. There's a reason the professionals do it in a garage on the lift, shoulder high. I set the flat tire to one side. The one advantage of a flat tire in this situation is that it won't roll away from you. On goes the limited use spare. And I'm missing a lug nut! I can only assume it washed away in the gutter. I get the others on and look for the missing piece. Finding no sign of it, I gave up. My day is over under any circumstances, and the tire will be fine down one nut, as long as I'm smart.

The car gets lowered to the ground; the nuts given a final tightening turn, and I dump everything into the truck. Not stowed the way my father taught me. Just dumped into the trunk. I will clean it up later. I climb back in the car, thank my rider again (who is very concerned about my condition, lol) and drop her off at home. I make my way home as well.

In case you're wondering, I got in touch with the service, and had the rider's trip adjusted. I appreciate her understanding, and it was the least I could do under the circumstances.

I'm also more careful going around corners these days.

CHAPTER NINE
By Neighborhood

Every city, town or village has better neighborhoods and rougher neighborhoods. They are not always what you expect. I will drive into any part of the metropolitan area where I work. Anywhere. And I have. I will never forget picking up a staffer at a local hospital, driving up into a rough part of town late at night. My rider told me, "As soon as you drop me off, you want to get out of this neighborhood as fast as you can." I took them at their word and headed back to more familiar territory.

In all the time I've driven I've never felt in danger. There was one time when I decided that a quick departure was in order based on what was happening around me. I had dropped off my rider near a complex of buildings when a young man came sprinting around the corner ahead of my position. No shirt, just sweat pants and his shoes. He wasn't running like he was trying to catch something. No, he was running like something (or someone) was trying to catch him. He was fleeing. What or why I will never know because I left the area, headed in the opposite direction.

Having said all that, there are differences between neighborhoods, and it comes down to income levels. As a sweeping generalization, the folks I pick up in the poorer parts of the city are more polite and more interesting to have in the car. I'm not saying that "rich people are rude". I've picked up plenty of people in the best neighborhoods in my area who have been polite, interesting, and a joy to take to their destination. But as a general rule, the folks in the "better" neighborhoods are more likely to ignore me than folks from other parts of the region. I'm providing a service, and there's no requirement for social interaction. They're not wrong, really. It's a matter of how a rider treats their driver. The worst situations are the times when folks, and ALL THE people in this category came from the upper-income neighborhoods, decide that I work for them, and have to do whatever they want. "Drive faster", "Go through this light", "I want the music louder". It's a tiny, tiny fraction of the two thousand plus riders I've had in my car, but they all come from the same neighborhoods. I'm not saying that every rider wants to be friends with me. I get riders from every neighborhood whose primary concern is getting home. But more often than not, if someone will be rude, I'm picking them up or dropping them off in the high price real estate districts.

I mention in the chapter on cancellations that some drivers try to limit the neighborhoods where they work. I can understand the concerns, but it's part of the business as far as I'm concerned. The only time I waver from that is when it comes to food deliveries. I've done some of that during the last couple years. But I turn that function off after nine thirty or ten o'clock. The reason is simple. I have no trouble driving into any neighborhood at eleven o'clock at night. I may not stick around long after the pickup or drop-off, but I'll go there. I don't like going into some neighborhoods late in the evening and getting out of my car. I never carry cash, and I have little of value on me when I'm driving (or any other time!). If someone wants my car, they can have it. If they want the food I'm delivering, my apologies to the customer but I'm handing that over too. I can replace things like cars and phones.

Having said all that, let me make one thing clear. I don't let neighborhoods make my decision on where I drive. The folks who call for a ride need one. The reasons may differ, but the need is the same. A broken car in the shop, an unexpected trip, not having a car at all, going shopping or getting to work. I'm always happy to help people have a good time and get home in safety. Many of my riders thank me for picking them up. They tell me that the service and I are blessings in their lives. What more could I hope for when the app chimes with another ride?

CHAPTER TEN
Navigational Errors

My biggest frustration with the ride share system is the navigation portion of the app. Before anyone gets too upset with me, let me note, the navigation system works fine 98% of the time. It shows me the fastest route and some alternates. I use a wireless earpiece and get the audio directions in my ear, which is a huge help when there's a lot of traffic. It means I can keep my eyes on the road and the crazy drivers around me. But it's not without flaws. That's one reason why you will find a backup GPS unit running while I'm driving. Two different views of the streets around me can solve problems quickly.

There's one quirk that shows up on a regular basis that I have never understood. I call it the "Behind The Building". For an unknown reason, the navigation will sometimes send me BEHIND the address listed. Not because the rider has requested it, just...because. Which means I find myself in alleys, or in parking lots on the far side of businesses. It's frustrating for everyone. After I had been doing this for a while, I knew what to look for on the map. My default is to go to the address given in the system, not the unexplained detour to God only knows where. That worked perfectly until late in my second year of driving. The system showed me in an alley behind the address, I ignored it and parked out front. Time passed and no one showed up. In a couple minutes the phone rang. It was my rider wondering where I was. Out front with my flashers on. They were in the alley. We had a good laugh about it when I picked them up.

It's not the only issue that crops up. I don't blame the system too much for this next one, however. Destinations in shopping center parking lots or apartment complexes can confuse the navigation as well. Each store has a street address, but they may not be anywhere near the street itself. Recently I had a call to a very large strip mall. It forms an enormous semi-circle around its massive parking lot. I carefully followed the directions the map was giving me, and ended up dead center in the parking lot! The nearest store was several hundred yards away. A quick call told which one I needed to go to and we were fine. It never hurts to give your driver a little extra information when you can. I love getting texts from riders telling me their precise location, what they are wearing, etc. It works to everyone's advantage.

The funniest navigation error has happened twice now, within a week of one another. The first was a pickup of a gentleman headed out to dinner a mile or so away. He was planning on having some fun, thought he might have more than was good for driving and was leaving the car at home. Perfect plan for a ride share! He climbed in and I waited for the system to spin up to speed and give me directions. I knew exactly where we were headed but getting the directions up on the screen is part of my routine. Except they didn't come up. The map was zooming in and out. In tight to the part of the city we were in, then out to most of the eastern half of North America. Back and forth and back and forth. I had never seen it do this before. So I asked the rider to double check his app to make sure he had put in the address properly. He acknowledged that it had been acting up for him too. At that moment, the system settled down and told me it couldn't give directions on trips that exceeded 1,000 miles.

Wait.

What?

We are still sitting at the curb at this point. I tell him that according to my app, he is going somewhere in northwestern Nebraska. Was that correct? (Yes, I just might have taken him if he'd said it was correct) Turns out it wasn't, somehow he had slipped up. Here's where it got weird. The system wouldn't let either of us change the destination! I finally offered to cancel the trip at my end, drive him to his destination and call it even. He was fine for that. I also told him that if the system charged him more than he thought the ride was worth (at this point I had no idea what charge might get spit out), he should challenge it and I would support him. The drive took about four minutes, and the amount that appeared on my screen when I dropped him off was what I would have expected for that drive. So it all ended well.

Then a week later, it happened again. Different part of town, I pick up a lady at her office, end of a long day, she's ready to kick back and relax. Navigation system begins that same weird zoom in/zoom out thing. But this time it's showing the Atlantic Ocean on the expanded view! We sat for a moment, waiting for it to settle down and I told her what had happened the week before. This time when it settled on a location, it was off the western coast of Africa! Hard to tell exactly, but it looked like somewhere near Liberia or the Cote D'Ivoire. I was going to have to take a pass on that one! This time the system let her change the destination, and I got her home without any major issues.

With the exception of the story I mention elsewhere, the navigation has never put me in the wrong place for a normal ride. I don't count the two long distance goofs because there was nothing normal about either of those situations. When I was just getting started, it was a vital partner. I was still new to my city and didn't know all the neighborhoods or streets. Having an "expert" riding along with me was a great confidence builder. Today, I know most of the city pretty well. It's still disturbing to me and the rider when the system decides not to be a good business partner!

CHAPTER ELEVEN
Professional Deafness

What do I hear?

That's a question that puzzles and bothers some of my riders. I say some because there is that small percentage who show no interest in me or even acknowledge my existence. My assumption is that it doesn't concern them if I hear anything.

Living in the age of smartphones, there's a lot that might get overheard. Not to mention conversations between people in the car. So let me set your minds to rest.

I call it "professional deafness". My bet is that most other drivers do as well. What is it? It means I'm not listening unless I know you are talking to me, or unless something catches my attention. To be honest, I'm driving surrounded by other moving vehicles, bicycles, pedestrians, potholes, construction, emergency vehicles, stop signs, traffic lights and God only knows what may pop up around the next corner occupying most of my attention. I'm not interested in most of what you're talking about.

On the other hand, this book proves I do remember some of what is said.

So, should you worry? That answer is easy. No. Even driving part-time, I will have between five and fifteen riders a day. That's an average of about fifty riders a week. I don't remember most of the details of any day's driving at the end of the same day. The same goes for the names of 99.9% of my riders, so I will not remember that YOU said something. I may remember if it was a male or a female, but there's no guarantee of that either.

So what is "professional deafness"? Think of it as selective hearing. I am alert to a rider talking to me. That is difficult if they are or have been on the phone. The folks who try to talk on the phone and give me directions make me crazy. It's rude, it's confusing and you're making life hard for us all. Please don't do this.

There are times when people talk to me as part of our "professional" relationship. The most common questions riders ask are "Can I/we...":

- Open a window (Absolutely)

- Talk on the phone (Of course!)

- Listen to music (Yes)

- Change the music on my radio (Probably)

- Change the setting on the heat/AC controls (Probably)

- Change their destination (Yes, go on the app and make the change)

- Add a stop (Same as above)

- Make an informal stop (Probably, if it's on the way. I try to be a nice guy)

- Eat (Please don't make a mess or leave stuff behind)

- Smoke/vape (No, sorry)

- Talk politics with me (Almost always no)

- Ask about driving for a ride-share service (Love to!)

- Ask for recommendations for bars, restaurants, sights to see (I can do that!)

- Time, temperature, weather or a thousand other details (I do what I can)

So I need to be listening for words intended for my ears. You wouldn't want a driver who is ignoring you, right? The goal is to find the balance between hearing and listening. For me that dividing line is paying attention. While you're talking most of what you're saying passes in one ear and out the other. I'm interested in a lot of things, so some conversation will perk up my ears. Here are a few examples:

- I picked you up at a club, bar, restaurant or event. You're talking about what happened, the food, the people. I'm listening to pick up information for other riders who may ask about that place or are looking for places like it.

- You are unsure of some local history, landmark, or some other form of trivia. I happen to love trivia and history, so I may offer the answer you need.

- You ask me my opinion on something. Which means I need to have some idea of what you were talking about!

I'm not "listening", in the sense that the information will be gone from my brain when you exit my car. But I am "hearing" almost everything that goes on in my car. On my way to the airport I hear lots of business conversations. Most of the time I do not understand what industry is being talked about, so I play a game in my head to guess. Since I never ask (because that would be rude), in most cases I never know if I was right. Those conversations are often in professional "jargon", the shorthand verbal communication that every line of work develops. You can say, "That Patterson thing" to a co-worker and they will know what you mean. Meanwhile, it's just words to me. One time I had two folks get in and discuss, in some detail, a development plan for part of the city.

Beyond that subject, I had no idea what they were talking about! It was like listening to a foreign language.

Some riders are worried about me hearing personal conversations. So they talk very, very softly. A couple things here. First, the inside of a car is a small space. So you have to be talking VERY softly to make sure that the driver doesn't hear. In my car, I am never more than five feet away from a rider. So past a certain level, not only can't I hear you, but the person you're talking to can't hear you either. Second, I am not interested in your personal life. I hope whatever relationship you have is happy, but I am not interested in the details. I only pay attention when something unusual happens. I've had two riders who were in the middle of painful conversations with their significant others. Not screaming arguments (had a couple of those too), but conversations about profound and painful issues. With just the two of us in the car on longer than average rides, it was impossible not to listen. Both apologized at the end of the ride. I told it wasn't a problem and wished them all the best. It was painful to listen to, and I still offer a little prayer for them now and then.

Most people are memory dumped as soon as they leave the car. And that's not a judgment on them. After thousands of riders, most rides are predictable. On the other hand, some folks make themselves memorable. I'm not going to apologize for remembering you then!

If the conversation you want to have is so delicate or secret, then you probably shouldn't have it with a witness around. But, at least in my car, you don't have to worry about the driver "listening".

CHAPTER TWELVE
Drunks of All Kinds

Any kind of rider might be a problem. One category, however, has built in issues that makes them one of the most dread inspiring riders out there. People who have been drinking. Folks who are a little drunk can be a blast. Those who are seriously drunk can be belligerent and have a high potential for making a mess. An unpleasant and expensive mess.

Even though I don't drive after midnight, I still get plenty of passengers who have been drinking. One of the best features of this entire industry is that allows grown ups to go out and have a good time, knowing they can get home in safety. I am not suggesting that this is an excuse for getting blackout drunk. The folks who do that don't need an excuse, but now there is an easy way to keep them off the highways. It's safer for us all. Not driving after midnight also means that the most egregious cases will ride in someone else's car. I like to tell people I will take them to the bar but they'll have to find a different ride home. Everyone seems to agree that it's a wise decision on my part.

But I still end up with drunks in my car. With over 2,000 rides I've had three people pass out in the back seat. Two of them were traveling with companions, so I had no trouble moving them out when we got to their destination. The one solo passenger woke up without extra effort when I turned on the dome light and spoke to him.

Think about that for a second. A passed out passenger, whether drunk or pooped, is something of a nightmare for the driver. The last thing anyone wants is to wake up to find a stranger's hand on them, no matter how innocent the intent. Picking up people at the end of a long work day who take a little snooze in the back seat is a regular event. I take it as a compliment. As a general rule, people will not fall asleep in a place where they don't feel safe. I want you to feel safe in my car. I also want to avoid people thinking I'm getting familiar. So when we are a couple minutes away from the destination, I will call out to the passenger. Most people are not in deep sleep so they wake right up and are thankful for the warning.

But back to the drunks now.

The more common kind of drunk is the one that has been having a good time and wants to share it with me. They are very chatty and very interested in me. In a vague, disjointed and often repetitious manner. Had one young person ask me the same question three times, in a row, within two minutes. Folks will upon occasion offer me one of the drinks they are carrying with them. I always decline. One young man said he enjoyed the ride so much that he thought I should come up to his apartment and have a drink with him. I declined that offer as well.

Drunks can also be belligerent. I've never had one get up in my face, but I watched three good friends go round and round at the pickup site. All three of them showed the effects of hours of drinking. Two of them were trying to convince the third he shouldn't drive home. He wanted no part of that. While never addressing me directly, he made it clear he didn't know me and would not ride with some stranger. The conversation that ensued was loud, obscenity-laden and long. Like 15-20 minutes long. (Confession time - once you come to my car, I start the ride. Which means I was "on the clock" with these folks for that entire time. The "per minute" charge is small, but I feel justified in getting paid something for this). There was no doubt that NONE of these three friends should be anywhere near a vehicle as a driver, but the one guy was not about to leave his car in a bar parking lot overnight. Which was not an unreasonable point of view. They called each other every name in the book, talked about how long they had known each other, told him they would pay for the whole thing. Nothing worked. We finally went on our merry way. I checked the local news for any crashes and didn't see one. So I'm hoping that he got home safe that night.

But my favorite drunk was one I picked up at a popular watering hole and took to his home, less than a mile away. He had been hitting it pretty hard and was in ultra-friendly mode. Lots of "conversation", most of which was how cool I was, and what a great driver I was, and how appreciative he was that I was giving him a ride home. As we pulled up in front of his house, he paused to think about his next statement.

"I love you, man."

I gave him a smile and thanked him.

"No, really. You're a great dude. I love you, man."

I felt a nudge at my shoulder. When I turned around, he had his hand out to shake. I took it, gave him a shake and he thanked me again. Then I reminded him we were at his destination and wished him a good night. He turned a bleary eye to the window to see that he was, in fact, home. Then he shook my hand again, wobbled his way out of the car, then leaned back in to say one more thing.

"You're the best. Love you, man."

If I have any questions about the condition of my riders, I try to keep an eye on them till they are at their door or inside the building. He got to the door without trouble, and I drove off into the night with a big smile on my face.

Easily, my favorite drunk.

CHAPTER THIRTEEN
Lost and Found

Things get left in the car. It's inevitable. When I'm driving at night, it's easy to overlook something that slides out of your pocket in the dark. The rider's focus is on their destination; home, work, party. So they pop out of the car looking ahead and not back. I always try to check the back seat before I roll on, but it doesn't always work. Even in the daylight, there are parts of the car I can't see. The foot-well and seat right behind me are blindspots. It's one reason I prefer people not ride there. If you're in the passenger side seats, front or rear, I can check to see if you've left anything behind. Then I can roll down the window and give a holler to let you know I have something you want.

But even with the best laid plans, things don't always work out.

The most common item left behind are keys. I find it curious that the most likely set of keys to for me to find are the ones connected to a big key ring or lanyard. You would think they would be obvious if you didn't have them, but time after time it's the keys I find.

Note on what to do if you realize that one of your belongings may still be in the car. Call the service and let them know. This puts it on the record and the provider will follow up with the driver. If you can contact the driver directly, do that second. From a driver's point of view, the goal is to get the item returned to you ASAP. The more time it takes is more time I'm not getting paid. With that in mind, remember that YOU left the item in my car. If I am in the middle of a delivery or a drive, I am not dropping everything to rush right back to you. I will take care of it as soon as I can, but sometimes that will be 15 minutes, 30 minutes or an hour. If you don't realize that it's missing till the next day, the return may be later than that. My personal standard is to do what I can as as soon I can. In the end, the problem is yours much more than it's mine. Sorry. Folks may think that sounds harsh, but I'm driving to pay my bills.

About a quarter of the time, they will contact me to look for the missing item and I won't find them. People are great about giving me items left by previous riders, so I don't think those items have "walked off". My theory has always been that they fell out as the rider was leaving the car. So your first move should be to go back to where I let you off and look there. When I do find them, I will get in touch with the service to let them know I have it. This involves sending a photo along with any information I may have on who the rider might have been. Your item may not show up right away. If it hits the floor and gets kicked under a seat, I may not find it for a day or two.

The vast majority of all items left in the car are returned. Clothing is the category that gets left behind and not claimed most often. Unless it's something special, people will abandon hats, shirts, sweatshirts, whatever. After a day or so, I donate them to a local charity.

My least favorite lost item is a cell phone. First, because it means the primary point of contact between you and me is sitting in my hand. Where it does neither of us any good. But the real reason this is my least favorite lost item is that I usually find it by having the crap scared out of me. Think about your ringtone, or the ringtones of some of your friends and acquaintances. Strange music, people singing or saying things. Now imagine driving at night, all by yourself and hearing that coming without warning from your backseat! I have had several heart attack inducing "discoveries" while I was driving. Take your phone, people!

There is one other item that I hate seeing show up in my car. A wallet. I've had exactly one wallet left behind and I shut down for the night till I could get it back to the owner. The reason has nothing to do with me being a good guy (OK, maybe a little), and a LOT to do with me not wanting to have your wallet. Cash, credit cards and ID all live there. And that makes people crazy. I try to avoid the crazy as much as possible.

The wallet in question was from a group of folks that I dropped off at a restaurant. I picked up another rider, and they handed the wallet over. As soon as I dropped off the new rider, I went offline to get this back to its owner ASAP. I opened it twice, to get and then double check the name and info on the driver's license. This information went to the service with the information about the time and location of the ride and rider. I heard from the service within minutes, and from the rider shortly thereafter. It ended up taking a couple minutes to re-connect, but I handed it over to them within 30 minutes of the loss. When I did, I asked them to double check the contents to verify that everything was there that should be. They were very cool about the whole thing, but I have never wanted to get rid of something as quickly in my whole life.

My favorite story about a lost item could have gotten me arrested. Or maybe shot. It was the weekend before Halloween, so a lot of grown-ups, including the local college students, were celebrating with costume parties. That meant I spent the evening driving various superheroes, monsters and strange characters around. They were all a lot of fun, including one group of four that included a young woman dressed as the comic character Lara Croft. She ended up in the front seat, next to me. They laughed and chatted and were a lot of fun to drive. An hour or so later, after multiple trips with smaller groups, I picked up two young men who wanted to go to Fort Lee. That's about 25 minutes from where I picked them up. It was late, the young men were rather uncommunicative other than saying hello and it all felt a little strange. Per my routine, I sent a quick text to my wife letting her know where to look for the body, in case I disappeared! (That's a tongue-in-cheek response, but bad things do happen. If I'm going way out of my normal "turf", I always let someone know.)

The ride down was uneventful. Once we were on the way, the two in back got a little chattier. At that point I discovered they were two young Marines headed to the military base at Fort Lee. When we arrived, I see a big gate, like in the movies. And like in the movies, there is a powerfully built sergeant with a sidearm in control of traffic. I grew up in a military family and learned long ago that you are always polite to non-commissioned officers. I greeted the sergeant, told him I had two of his to drop off. He gave me instructions on leaving them inside the gate. As I dropped them off, I did my routine check of the backseat. Clear. As I turned back to the front my eyes fell on what was in the front seat. It seems that "Lara Croft" had dropped her chrome-plated .45 caliber toy pistol when she got out earlier in the evening. There it was, sitting in the seat as big as life. And I had just carried it onto a U.S. military base! The sergeant had taken my ID when I'd driven on the base, so I had to stop again to get out. I swept the toy under the seat and left without incident.

I can only assume that the sergeant saw it, it was dead center in the seat and the lights were bright at the gate. The orange safety tip was visible too. But I'm surprised that he didn't call me on it. I had the cold sweats for about fifteen minutes afterward!

Contacted my wife to let her know all was well, and that I'd have a good story to share that night.

So do yourself and your driver a favor next time you ride share. Make sure everything that came with you, leaves with you!

CHAPTER FOURTEEN
Bad Driver

I am sorry to say I sometimes hear stories about bad behavior by drivers. It's inevitable that some drivers involved in these services aren't the cream of the crop. People sign up only to discover that they don't have the personality for it, they have a bad experience, or they are just not nice people. It happens. The problem is that until they leave the program, riders will get stuck with them. Which will color their attitude toward all the drivers that follow. Like me. Which is why I work very hard to make sure you have a great ride with me. For my own sake (love those five star ratings!) and for all the other drivers out there.

Let me be clear here, if you have a bad experience with a driver, tell the ride share company. For minor problems give a less than five star review. For major issues, file a complaint. Don't wait. Don't feel guilty. As a ride share driver, I don't want those people screwing up the system or the market. I want them gone, and so should every other driver out there. You should feel confident you will get a safe, comfortable and, as much as possible, enjoyable ride, every time you get into a ride share car.

The overwhelming majority of riders I talk to have positive things to say about their experience with ride share drivers. There is a small percentage of stories that involve drivers behaving in ways that are not acceptable.

Some stories I've heard:

Drivers who are rude. This is a customer service industry job. The number of stories I have heard about drivers who don't like being around other people astounds me. While a job that would put me in the company of other people without a break would wear me out, this job is people followed by a period of me all by myself. Then, (I hope!) more people! Yet, I've heard stories about drivers who tell riders "I don't do small talk". Ones that made it clear the rider was little more than a package to be delivered. You're here, get out. One advantage of this work is that you make your own schedule. Having a bad day? Skip work. Had a PITA rider and you're in a foul mood? Turn the app off and cool off. But if you don't like people, this is not the job for you.

One of the fun things about driving, at least for me, is that I meet all kinds of people. I have met a former mayor of the city, and I have met dancers at local men's clubs. If memory serves I have driven three young women I know were dancers (they told me so) and a couple others who might have been. All wonderful, polite and fun riders to have in my car. One asked if she could sit up front to use the visor mirror because she was running late and hadn't finished her makeup! You go, girl! But she was also the one who told me the story about the driver who decided she was pretty and so he would take her to his house. She knew how to handle out of line guys (professional skill, I'm sure). She told him, in no uncertain terms, exactly what would happen if he didn't stop the car that instant and let her out. Wisely, he followed instructions. But this kind of behavior is the kind you should report, not only to the ride service but to the cops. Get away from this predator, get a photo of the car license if you can and/or him, and call another driver, a friend or a cop.

The list of people through my car doors includes people from all over the the world. There are lots of international students here, but I also met a refugee who came to the is country and created a successful business for himself. I've met NFL players, teachers, fast food workers, international business people, and people fighting life-threatening health battles. Every one of them deserves the same level of efficient, polite service. Every one, every time. It is my belief that most drivers deliver that every day.

Every driver I have ever spoken to has stories about the navigation system making a mistake. It comes with the territory. I talk about my own experiences elsewhere in the book. One lady had found a strange quirk in the system. She worked at let's call it 3000 North Main Street. When she requests a ride, the navigation system directs the driver to 3000 South Main Street. She told me this when she got in to make sure it was right this time. Nope. Directed me to the wrong end of the street. And we are talking several miles apart. Here's where the bad driver comes in. The last driver took her to the wrong address, and told her he had another ride lined up and she had to get out! I couldn't believe my ears. Yes, this is a tough situation for the driver. The only way around it for the driver was to cancel the second ride (lost income, and a rating down mark). No driver wants to do that. I would suggest doing it and then contesting the demerit with the service later. But I'm an eternal optimist. He wouldn't budge. This is where the system said she was to go and he got her there. Get out. In my opinion, it's a jerk move. I put my app into "Last Ride" mode and promised her to get her to work. And I did. As the saying goes - that's the way I roll. I can not imagine dropping a rider off in the middle of nowhere, when that isn't where they want to go. Which is why I never do it. As I'm writing this, there's a story in the news about a driver who decided that he didn't want to take the rider to the destination. This was AFTER he had picked her up and driven her miles into the middle of nowhere. He pulled over and told her she had to get out. I was very happy to read that the rider got home safely and that the driver was banned from the service. Unacceptable behavior.

Would I ever stop mid-ride and tell a rider to get out? Yes. If they became abusive to me or another rider. Or if they were involved in a criminal activity in my car. Can't think of any other instance.

My goal is simple, to get you where you want to go quickly, safely and enjoyably. That may mean talking about whatever is on your mind. Or it may mean driving in silence and leaving you alone with your thoughts. At the end of the ride, I want you to be able to say the ride was what you wanted it to be.

Let me stress again, if a driver doesn't behave the way you think they should, let the appropriate people know. All I ask is that you remember we're human too and sometimes have bad days. But if your driver steps over the line, you're doing everyone a favor by letting the system know.

CHAPTER FIFTEEN
Long Trips

A ride share driver's life is defined by two things - time and distance. The time and distance of our paid rides and the time and distance BETWEEN those paid rides. A long ride pays well and we all love those. A long ride that takes us into an area that where we are unlikely to find another ride, not so much. The time to get back to where the rides are is dead time. In the railroad industry it's called "dead heading". I think it's the same for truckers. I'm burning gas, adding miles to the wear and tear on my vehicle, and not making any money. That's not a look any driver likes.

So some drivers do everything they can to avoid long trips. It makes life hard for folks who live away from the urban centers. There is little public transportation available in these areas, and cab or livery services can be very expensive. So the ride share services could be the answer to a prayer for these folks. But then you run into the time and distance problem. The time I have to spend to get to the pickup is a total loss for me. Since I'm doing this to make money, that's a problem.

The solution many drivers adopt is to do everything they can to avoid long trips. If they pickup is too far a way, they decline. The app will let us know in advance if it is a long trip (45+ minutes). Many drivers will decline those. That way they can get as many rides in the prime target area as possible. I understand the logic, but I also feel for the needs of the rider.

There's a lot of "countryside" near the city where I drive. I get grumpy when a ride takes me way out there when I know I won't get another ride till I've driven a long way back. My attitude changes a little based on the time of day. I only drive for a certain number of hours on any day. If I'm going to get a long ride out of town, I want it to happen as soon as I get started, or right when I'm ready to quit. One at the beginning still gives me time to get caught back up. And it starts the day with a nice big addition to my earnings. At the end of my day, I want one headed toward home. For the record that almost never happens. If it's almost time to get home, that long trip will be in the exact opposite direction. Sigh.

I've only had two long, long trips, both north towards our nation's capitol. The good news is that I made good money on each one. The first one was enough it was a clear profit over even a good hour, in fact, it rivaled my best hours ever. I picked up a rider on the east side of town and drove almost two hours north. He was very pleasant, and we had a great conversation for the trip. We talked about the economics of what he was doing. He'd looked at bus, train, cab and plane travel. None of them could beat the combination of cost and time that the ride share offered. He set the schedule, unlike the more common ways to travel. The trip was simpler and much, much less expensive. If memory serves, his cost was around $130 (out of which my cut was over $90). With what I had already earned that day, I was set. The drive home was boring, but I was OK. I could have stuck around and done trips up there but that comes with all kinds of problems. I don't know the neighborhood, it's late at night, and it was the end of the day. By the time I got home, it was after one in the morning. It made for a long, long day.

The other long trip was similar, with another destination more than an hour north. It was not as long, so the profit wasn't quite as high. Still, for the time I spent on the road, it averaged out to some of my more profitable hours.

There have been a few occasions when I've taken a long ride out of town, usually to a "destination" (a brewery or amusement park) and gotten lucky. I picked up a second ride, back into town! Those are days are treasures. You are making money in both directions and getting two longer trips as well! One trip that wasn't as long (only about 40 minutes) turned into a good night. I dropped the rider off at their destination and prepared myself for the deadhead ride home. Then I got a call for a short ride in the direction I was going! Great! Dropped them off and a few minutes later got a second call, also going that same direction! I ended up stringing three shorter trips together that got me back to where I wanted to be with a minimum of "dead" time. It doesn't happen as often as I'd like.

As I mention in a different chapter, there is nothing worse than a long pickup that results in a cancellation. The cancellation fee that the driver receives isn't large enough to make up for the wasted time. I'm not sure there's an easy answer to the problem, except to create a new category with a higher price. Finding the balance between what the market will bear and a reasonable profit margin for the driver will be the hard part.

If you need a pickup that requires a long drive to get you, or if you need a ride to a distant destination, please remember your driver is going above and beyond the normal service. A tip would be great, at the least make sure they know how much you appreciate them.

CHAPTER SIXTEEN
The Victimless Cheat

There is a basic human urge to get an advantage. I have done it myself. The urge to do it is stronger in some people than others. When the system being gamed belongs to an anonymous corporation, most of us don't even feel guilty about doing it.

In the case of the rideshare system, there are two groups affected if a rider tries to game the system. One is a big, anonymous corporation. I'm not advocating for trying to game them. They've created a very cool system that works well overall. They have every right to expect to get paid for that work.

The other group are the drivers. I've mentioned before that we drive to make money. Maybe it's pocket money for fun stuff, or maybe it's paying our bills. Either way, we are making ourselves and our vehicles available to take you where you want to go. In return, we have every right to get paid for our time and effort.

Most of my riders have no trouble with this at all. As I mention elsewhere, I not only get thanks from my riders, many of them mention that the service is a blessing in their life. That statement comes in many forms, but it means the same thing-thank you for being there when I needed/wanted you. I appreciate the sentiment. It's nice to feel appreciated.

Some riders will try to game the system. I'm sure they think they are just sticking it to the big corporation, but the reality is that they are sticking it to their driver as well. Some folks who have done what I'm about to describe aren't trying to rip off the driver. I believe that they haven't thought about the consequences, or think there aren't any. Remember that a driver's day is governed by time and distance. It's how we get paid. So if the rider starts playing with those parameters it's a problem.

The first example of someone gaming the system is the "quick stop". I try to be a nice guy, but there are times when this gets out of hand. If you want to make a quick stop some place that's on the route, I will try to accommodate you. Not all drivers will. They're not being mean, it's a business decision. Here's the time and mileage equation again. At the moment I write this I get paid approximately twelve cents a minute while you're in the car. The rate for mileage is approximately sixty-five cents a mile. So I'm better off when I'm moving. If I'm stopped, my payment rate isn't to my advantage.

The other issue with the "quick stop" is that it almost never is quick. My busiest times are rush hours. Which means everyone and their brother/sister is out and about. Which means that the banks and stores are jammed with customers. So telling me you're just going to run in real fast and be right back is beyond your control. Most of my stops are five minutes or fewer. That doesn't make me happy, but it's a business decision I have made in the light of good customer service. But I agreed to stop so one older lady could run in and get a space heater because the furnace was out at her house in mid-winter. Fine, I'll be the good guy and helpout. One minute became five, five became ten, ten became fifteen. At this point, I'm thinking about bailing. Except she was a very nice old lady who has trouble getting in and out of my car. She needs the service more than most. But this was costing me money. I'm making twelve cents a minute instead of working a whole new ride. At the twenty-minute mark she finally shows up. The store was busy, they had the model she needed, but it was in the back and no one could get back there. Then there was a problem with the payment machine. None of it my rider's fault. All of it was a problem for me.

The folks who really annoy me are the ones who intentionally try to get something for nothing. They are the ones who want to make a serious detour, one that takes us well off the planned route. That changes both time and mileage and should change the cost of the ride. The hope is that they can get a longer ride without paying for it. And that's bad business for me. The other version of this that I hear regularly is when I have more than one rider for the trip. As I approach the (only) destination listed they ask if I could take one of the riders to a different destination that's "not too far away". If it's a block or two, I'll be the nice guy and do it. Any more than that and I will ask them to add the new destination to the trip. The issue can be that the system shows me as having reached my destination. So it begins to search for new rides for me. Adding "unscheduled" stops at the end of the ride can slow me down and potentially cost me money.

Multi-stop trips are part of the system and it's not hard to program in. And it can be done up to the end of the ride. Some folks are a little intimidated by the app, so I tell them to wait till we're a minute or so away from the end, then just change the final destination.

Most folks are good about this. As I said, I don't think most of them realize that they are creating an issue for the driver. If they realize that they are "cheating" the system, they probably think it's a victimless cheat. While not perfect, the system is pretty good.

CHAPTER SEVENTEEN
Big Tipper!

There is nothing more enjoyable than glancing at your total for the day, looking away and then glancing back to see the number has jumped by a couple dollars. It means I got a tip. Getting five star reviews from my riders is important, but it doesn't match the pleasure of getting a tip.

Let's be clear, no one driving for a ride share company is getting rich. On a per hour basis, the pay can be pretty low. Add in the mileage, and wear and tear on your car, and it takes a lot of driving to make the process profitable. I've been a rider twice, and I always take the opportunity to chat about driving. On my last ride, the driver told me he was working full time. He bought a newer car for the gig and tracked his expenses very closely. The income was designed to supplement his retirement. So he knew how much money he had to make every day to pay for his car expenses and make the amount of money he needed to get the income he wanted. Some days it was 8 hours of driving to get there. Other days could be 12 hours or longer. My bet is that every driver has some standard they need to achieve on a daily or weekly basis. I know I do.

So tips can be a big help in getting to that goal. I'm not going to tell you that you should tip every driver. If the trip wasn't satisfactory, why would you tip them? But I would ask you to consider adding a small tip to any trip that went well. A dollar tip added to each of my trips would get me home sooner every day. My personal goal is weekly, so if I get at least a $1 tip from the 40 or so rides I average, that $40 closer to my goal without having to work longer hours.

Right about now my fellow drivers are tearing their hair out. Because we all get tips above the $1 level. I am NOT saying you shouldn't tip more than that. If you already tip your driver, keep doing what you're doing. A driver who answers questions, gets your to where you need to be on time, or goes out of their way to help you out (those quick unscheduled stops as an example), should get a the extra "thank you" represented by a tip. I'm thinking more in terms of the riders who don't normally tip. For my riders, I would say 60-70% of my rides don't result in a tip. Some folks might believe that's a representation of my service, but my rating is consistently very high, so I don't believe that. Most of my rides are short. Folks taking short rides don't think about leaving a tip. In many cases, I know that money is tight for them because we discuss why they are taking the ride. I appreciate money being tight. I'm suggesting that adding a dollar when you can could go a long way to making life more pleasant all round.

When I do get tips, they fall into the $1-$5 range as a rule. Tips were an issue in the industry at the beginning, with one service including a way to tip in the app and the other not doing so. Today, you can add a tip right in the app. With some updates, there is even a way to set a standard tip! Most of my tips come through the app, but about 25% of them are cash. Years ago, I worked as a bell hop at a vacation hotel. What the senior staff taught me was to NEVER look at the tip in front of the customer. It's a habit I still maintain. If you let me know you're going to give me "a little something" I will thank you, glance your way to see your hand, accept whatever you hand me, and stick it into the center console of the car without a glance. The check will come after you're out and I'm on my way. I never judge a rider on the size of a tip. You tipped me! I am very happy with you.

Some tips are bigger than others. I had one rider whose pickup spot was out of the way, and needed a ride with stops and that took a while to achieve. They promised me a nice tip, and followed through. It makes me glad that I accepted the trip, even though it was a long way out of my way.

There is one category of rider that I know is never going to tip me. Even though they promise a tip more often than not. Riders who have been drinking. As I mention in the chapter on drunks, these riders can be very friendly. And they want me to know that they will take care of my tip as soon as they get inside. I smile. It never happens. Ever. It's OK, I understand.

Two stories about tipping, one bad and one good. Bad one first.

This was early in my driving career, before you could tip on the app. I picked up some riders at an industrial site. Based on the conversation, they were engineers from out of town. When we arrived at their hotel, the one rider realized he only had a $10 bill. He got annoyed that I didn't have change. The ten dollar bill was way too much tip for the length of the ride, and I told him it was OK. But he insisted on giving me the tip, all while being irritated with me. The feeling I got was that he thought I was taking advantage of him, somehow. I rarely carry cash, even in everyday life. Being able to tip in the app solves this issue once and for all.

Are you wondering what my biggest tip was? That's story number two. The pickup was in an unremarkable part of the city. The ride was a couple miles into downtown, maybe three miles and maybe 6 minutes. As typical a ride as you can imagine. The rider was chatty and chose to sit up front with me. Turns out he was a successful entrepreneur with a small, thriving local business. We chatted about various subjects and at some point I noted that we have a rule in my family about making dumb decisions. We are a tight knit group and are always there for each other. But the rule is that there is no sympathy for self inflicted wounds. If you do something dumb, something you should have known better than to do, and it messes you up, then expect no sympathy. That simple concept appealed to him. Enough for him to ask me to repeat it so he would be sure to remember it. I thought that was cool and a little strange at the same time. We pulled up in front of his destination and he said he wanted to give me a little something as thanks for the pleasant ride. Per my practice I thanked him and accepted the bill he handed me. I never look. That's the rule. But this time the corner of the bill was clearly visible. A one followed by two zeroes. I confess, I gawked. Then I asked him if he was sure he had given me the right bill. He told me that he had enjoyed the ride and had learned something along the way. Life was treating him well and he made it a habit to pass some of that along. I thanked him again. And then took a break, to wrap my head around what had happened.

Very few of us are in a position to drop that kind of tip. But it's a great example of sharing to the degree we all can. All I'm asking is if a dollar tip might be something you can do. Thanks for considering the idea, and I won't take offense if the answer is no.

CHAPTER EIGHTEEN
Making Your Ride Safe

I wish I didn't have to include this chapter. But stories about both riders and drivers assaults crop up in the news on a regular basis. In the best of all possibleworlds, the system would work smoothly. Riders would request a ride, a driver would pick them up, they would share some polite conversation, arrive at the destination and bid each other a nice day. In my ownexperience, that is the overwhelming majority of rides. As I've noted before, I get the occasional cranky person, but no other issues.

The news tells me how lucky I am.

To be clear, this chapter is about the "worst-case scenario" ride. A situation where you do not feel safe in the car. Where something is happening, that is making you worried or afraid. A driver (or rider) can be a jerk, without making you feel unsafe. There is a line where actions move from uncomfortable to unsafe. It varies from person to person. If you think you can resolve the situation, I urge you to try. But if you are afraid, take action to assure your own safety.

The stories about violence and sexual assaults represent a tiny portion of the rideshare industry. If they didn't, the entire industry would have collapsed by now. In my conversations with my riders, I know there is another level of bad behavior below the violence that is a problemas well. There's no way to guarantee you will be safe in every circumstance (you could be the victim of a crime walking down the street), but here are a few ideas to help you be as safe as possible in your rideshare.

It should start before you get in. Your app will provide you with lots of information about the driver picking you up. Model and color of the car, license plate, the driver's name and photo. All of my photos come out awful, so don't judge your driver too much by that. Check the car, check the license, and then do one more thing:

Before you get in, ask the driver "Ride for who?" (or whom if you're a grammar fanatic). Your driver has some information about you as well. They should be able to give you the name on the account that called for the ride. Under normal circumstances, that's the name on your account, but if someone is providing a ride for you, know that name. To help the driver know that you're the right rider, know their name too. But make sure they have the correct name before you get in.

(Note: one of the other behaviors I want you to avoid are drivers who are angry, belligerent and rude. Some drivers get impatient if the rider doesn't leap into the car. This kind of driver may get rude when you ask the question above. Tell them you want to make sure it's the correct ride. If they continue to be rude and refuse to tell you, or say they'll tell you after you get rolling, my advice is-Don't get in. Cancel the ride, give them a low rating and make sure the app company knows what happened. Yes, it will be a hassle, but it's better than getting into a car with a belligerent stranger.

Please understand, drivers worry about our safety too. Drivers are assaulted, groped and carjacked. We want to do as many rides as we can, providing a safe and pleasant way for people to get from Point A to Point B. Keeping my eye on a sketchy rider in back is scary and unsafe. The more I have to pay attention in the back, the less attention I'm paying to the road. If we both take routine precautions, the system will work.

As long as we are talking about safety, let's take a moment to talk about young people in my car. The rules of the app are clear, no riders under 18 without an accompanying adult. As a former youth minister, I understand and agree with this rule. Calling a rideshare for you kid on a day when you can't get there may seem like no big deal. But you put that young person in a vehicle with a person neither your nor they know. Yes, we undergo basic background checks, but I stress the word, basic. Once they climb in, the driver is in complete control of where your child goes. Yes, most drivers would deliver your child safely. But, as I noted at the beginning, the news features stories about what the tiny minority does regularly. Plus, it is against the rules for a driver to pick up such a rider. We canbe banned from the app for doing this. I HATE leaving a young person stranded, but I still need this gig, and I don't need the potential headaches that come with going against the system. Do us all a favor and don't ask me to do it.

The other safety issue is with small children. The law about safety seats still applies. I'm a safe driver with a sterling record, but there are lots of idiots out there. I can't control when they will crash into me. Make sure your child isproperlysecured when they ride in my car. It may add a minute or two to each end (always the nice guy, I tend to not start the ride till the child is secure, and end it while you are getting child and chair out of my car), but it's so important that you do everything you can to keep your children safe.

I mention this other places in the book, but I want to say it again. If your driver is making you feel unsafe, GET OUT OF THE CAR AS SOON AS POSSIBLE. Depending on the level of your concern, don't be afraid to contact the app, call a friend to let them know what's happening or even call 9-1-1. Once you are out, move away from the car to the nearest safe area. Call for another ride, or whatever you feel is appropriate. Stay aware of what's happening around you (has the driver turned around and headed back towards you?). When you are safe, make sure you give the driver a low rating and contact the app with a complaint. A driver that makes you feel unsafe isn't one we need in the system. The same thing goes for drivers. If there is a problem, I try to resolve it. But there's a line for me. Riders that make me feel unsafe don't need to be in the system. If I don't feel safe with you in my car, I will tell you to get out. If you don't, I will shut the car down, put on the flashers, take my phone and get out myself. At that point, I will be calling 9-1-1. Once I feel safe, it's a low rating and complaint to the service.

As I said at the beginning, all of this covers a very tiny percentage of rides. I want you to never have to use any of these tips. But I want you to have this in the back of your mind, in case you ever need them.

CHAPTER NINETEEN
Tips to a Better Ride

Here are my tips on making your next ride easier and more enjoyable.

1: **Be Ready.** Nothing makes a driver crankier than arriving at the pickup and there's no rider in sight. There are times when we show up sooner than you expect. But generally it takes a couple minutes to get from where we get the notification to where you are. When I'm waiting, I'm not making any money. If you are running late, then go to Tip #2.

2: **Communicate!** A quick text or call to let your driver know what's happening can smooth a lot of rough edges. Both major services offer text and phone links to your driver. If there's a problem, if you're in an unusual location, heck, just let me know what you're wearing so I can find you quicker, let me know! Communication after you're in the car is a great help too. Let me know if there is something you need, rather than just giving me a bad rating.

3: **Use The App For Trip Changes.** Don't just ask me to detour. I will take you where you need/want to go. But I expect to be paid fairly for it. Want to make a quick stop some place on the route? Usually not a problem. Want to make a major change in the trip? Plug it into the app so I get paid for the time and distance.

4: **Be Polite.** If you don't want to have a conversation with your driver, that's fine. But a hello when you get in and a thank you at the end isn't too much to ask. If you need to talk on the phone, also cool. Just make sure your driver knows when you're talking on the phone and when you're talking to me.

5: **If You Want To Navigate The Trip, Then Navigate.** Some folks believe they know a better way to get to where we're going. I'm usually OK with that. The folks who tell me not to follow the navigation, then jump back into the phone conversation are frustrating. If you leave me without further directions, I will go back to following navigation. Don't get crabby because I'm not going the way you think I should if you're not engagedin the process. And remember what I said in the chapter on navigation-you may think you know a better way, but you probably don't.

6: **Respect My Car And My Rules.** Please don't leave a mess behind. I've found trash and drinks (the open beer can was not cool) left in my car. Worse yet are when they are out of my line of sight and my next rider finds them. If you ask to do something (like vaping) and I say no, then it's no. Don't tell me it will fine. It's not.

7: **Give me 60 seconds of your attention at the start of the ride.** It may not take that long, but that's when we need to do a little basic communication. Like making sure this is the correct car for you, any special issues or questions, etc. More and more riders get in with their earbuds in and don't hear me. Give me a minute (or less) and I can make the process better for us both.

8: **Sit Where You Like, But...** In my car you can sit in front or back. Not all drivers like having single riders up front, so refer to Tips #6 and 7. I have only one request about where you sit. If you are a single rider, please don't sit right behind me. It makes it harder to communicate with you, and honestly, it's a little creepy.

9: **Check Before You Leave The Car.** The best way to make sure you don't lose something is to check your seat before I pull away. I will do a quick checkas well, so there is time. Everybody's day goes better if you leave with everything you came with.

10: **TIP!** Even if it's just a dollar. Reward the driver who does a good job for you. It's one of the best ways to make sure that good drivers keep driving and offering great service.

CHAPTER TWENTY
Author Bio

Author Bio

J. D. Phillippi

A lifelong storyteller, J. D. Phillippi draws on a diverse career and vivid imagination for source material in his writing. From dishwasher to radio talk show host, bell hop to Episcopal youth minister, he brings a depth of understanding to characters at every level of society. Whether writing short stories or in novel length works, Phillippi weaves stories that draws the reader into the moment.

Born near Pittsburgh, Pennsylvania, Phillippi lived most of his life in the western part of the state. He attended Edinboro State College (now Edinboro University), a few miles south of Erie, PA, where he took a degree in Liberal Arts (Theater). While there he helped to put WFSE-FM on the air at the college. He worked as an announcer, Program Director, and General Manager during his time there. Following graduation, Phillippi pursued a career in radio. Beginning as a News Editor/Newscaster at WASP-AM in Brownsville PA, his storytelling abilities saw him quickly move into a full-time airshift. Phillippi became the station's morning man in less than two years. Radio would take him to Erie, PA and then Jamestown, NY working almost exclusively in drive time airshifts.

Just shy of 20 years into his radio career, Phillippi answered a call to join the staff of the Bishop of the Episcopal Diocese of Western New York as Diocesan Youth Missioner. He served there for 13 years before taking a job in congregational ministry in Richmond, VA. Since then he published his first book, (the short story collection "Shorts"), worked as a substitute teacher in a local school district, an Uber/Lyft driver, and audiobook narrator. He wrote, voiced and produced an independent media commentary radio program for a decade.

Married to his college sweetheart, Phillippi lives outside Richmond, VA and enjoys the many attractions in the area. Their only child is also an author, published under the name K Orion Frey ("Son of the Revolution").

CHAPTER TWENTY-ONE
Other Works

Other Books By J.D. Phillippi
"Shorts-A Collection of Short Fiction"

Sixteen stories explore everything from the "true" story behind a popular song to Earth's first encounter with an alien race, your deepest fears of childhood and a grown man's dark fantasy. Spanning genres, "SHORTS" offers moments of quiet reflection, terror, sadness, and humor. It's the perfect book for a snatched moment of reading or a quiet weekend. Enter into the author's self-described "vivid imagination" and enjoy the stories that are waiting for you there.

- First Contact finally happens, and Earth doesn't like or understand what happens.

- Being trapped by a snowstorm is never fun. Being trapped inside with some thing that is making horrifying noises is worse.

- The characters in a young man's favorite video suddenly go on strike.

- The final moments of two lives together, and a decision that has to be made.

- A funny look at reality behind a legend.

- Trying to re-connect with family tradition and the soil.

Plus 10 more stories!

What Readers Have Said About "Shorts" -

"I thoroughly enjoyed these stories...a perfect read for those times you know you won't have a lot of time to read"

"Quirky and Good"

"Shorts is a delightful short fiction collection by J.D Phillippi that spans both genres and ecades. Phillippi's rich language paints vivid images of the people and places throughout the collection."

"I've read one or two per day because I do no want it to end!"

CHAPTER TWENTY-TWO
Contact Me!

I'd love to hear from rideshare riders and drivers! If you've never been involved with rideshare, but enjoyed the stories, drop me a line. If you thought the whole thing was kinda dumb, let me know as well. You can reach me a variety of places, including:

My website : JDPhillippi.com

This is "home base" for all my writing. You'll find links to my blogs and Twitter feeds, plus information about my books, the audiobooks I've narrated for other authors, and other projects I'm doing.

Email : JDPhillippiAuthor@Gmail.com

Found a mistake? Have a story to share? Feel free to drop me a line. I will answer as I can, but I'm working multiple jobs these days, so it may take a while.

Twitter : @phlipsidejdp

All my tweets associated with my writing and other creative pastimes. Some funny stuff, some serious too.

Facebook : www.facebook.com/phlipsidecreative

Another place to keep track of what's going on. Activity tends to come in bursts.

CPSIA information can be obtained
at www.ICGtesting.com
Printed in the USA
LVHW110207191219
641050LV00001B/88/P